Mistaking Each Other for Ghosts

Longlist Finalist for the National Book Award
and one of the *New York Times* ten "Best Poetry Books of 2015"

"Raab brings a darker timbre to poetry's comfortable middle register; his eminently approachable, low-key lines are never quite as affable as they seem, and the book is all the better for that." —**David Orr**, *New York Times Sunday Book Review*

"These poems offer powerful evocations of the most human of themes: loneliness, the haunting resolution of doubt, love's many shades, and a deeply intelligent form of comfort amid the messiness of emotions. Always, reason balances high sentiment and dramatic outbursts. Raab's is a wholly American voice that reveals itself in sardonic humor and reflection as the poet addresses universal, philosophical quandaries; heaven and hell; and everything in between. . . . A wonderful, mature, sweeping collection." —**Mark Eleveld**, *Booklist*

"Raab . . . exhibits tight lyricism and a characteristically American wit in meditations on mortality and intimacy. . . . [W]ild swings in tone and subject matter are common throughout. . . . What binds this collection is neither the formal qualities of the poems, nor Raab's unmistakable voice, but his ability to move across registers with consistency and well-tempered feeling." —*Publishers Weekly*

"Pretend that these poems by Lawrence Raab have come to you from very far away. Think of them as written by Poet Z, a heretofore-unheard-of Eastern European poet, a Kafka-Andrade-Calvino character from Serbo-Chechnya-Lithuania.

What's in his poems? Angels and human monsters, decades and generations, universities turned into ashes, the consolation of philosophy, despair in the middle of the night, a tutorial in lucid dreaming.

Now, these poems by Z have finally been translated into an American idiom that is canny, sly, defeated, pessimistic, resilient, and perplexingly knowledgeable about the human predicament. They are also often beautiful, bewildered, disquieting, and full of paradoxical laughter and contemplative solace. *Mistaking Each Other for Ghosts* is a tender, lonely, deeply intelligent tour of that distinctive country of the soul." —**Tony Hoagland**

"I don't know anything like Lawrence Raab's poems. I can't get anything like this voice from anywhere else, and that is very rare. 'A Cup of Water Turns into a Rose,' the long poem that concludes *Mistaking Each Other for Ghosts*, is spellbinding—intricate and resonant in its weave, and very strange in its clarity and the odd lucid story it seems to be telling and untelling. The more I read it, the poem seems absolutely extraordinary; somehow of a piece with Lawrence Raab's recent writing, but also unlike anything I have read." —**Adam Phillips**

Also by Lawrence Raab

Mistaking Each Other for Ghosts

Poems by
Lawrence Raab

Tupelo Press
North Adams, Massachusetts

Mistaking Each Other for Ghosts.
Copyright © 2015 Lawrence Raab. All rights reserved.

Library of Congress Cataloging-in-Publication Data
Raab, Lawrence, 1946–
[Poems. Selections]
Mistaking each other for ghosts : poems / by Lawrence Raab.
   pages ; cm
ISBN 978-1-936797-65-3 (pbk. : alk. paper)
I. Title.
PS3568.A2A6 2015
811'.54--dc23
              2015017797

Cover and text designed by Howard Klein, set in Monotype Centaur.
Cover art: Mary Frank, "Amaryllis" (c. 1976), monoprint, 37 ½ by 25 inches. Courtesy of DC
Moore Gallery, New York (www.dcmooregallery.com).

First paperback edition: September 2015.

Tupelo Press
P.O. Box 1767, North Adams, Massachusetts 01247
Telephone: (413) 664–9611 / editor@tupelopress.org / www.tupelopress.org

Tupelo Press is an award-winning independent literary press that publishes fine fiction,
nonfiction, and poetry in books that are a joy to hold as well as read. Tupelo Press is a registered
501(c)(3) nonprofit organization, and we rely on public support to carry out our mission of
publishing extraordinary work that may be outside the realm of the large commercial publishers.
Financial donations are welcome and are tax deductible.

ART WORKS.
arts.gov

Supported in part by an award from the National Endowment for the Arts

for Judy as ever

Contents

4

You know then that it is not the reason
That makes us happy or unhappy.
— *Wallace Stevens*

Just because you feel it doesn't mean it's there.
— *Radiohead*

O, how wrong things sparkle . . .
— *Vic Chesnutt*

Riddle

from the Anglo-Saxon

All that I am keeps me silent
as I step among the grasses
or trouble the water. Sometimes
I'm lifted by the high winds far above
your houses, and when the sweep
of clouds carries me away you may think
you can hear my song—how clear
and strange it is—the voice of a being
traveling alone and far from sleep—
a spirit, a ghost, no one like yourself.

I

Once, But No Longer

Let's say you feel someone is better off
dead, but you don't do anything about it.
That could be a sign of civilization—
how you're able to manage such admirable
restraint. Say it's Sunday, so you amble

down to your garden where the cruelties
of life almost vanish. Here
you can tell what needs to be uprooted
or carefully tended. You understand
what must be left alone. This may not be

the case the next time you meet Frank
at the office and you think, Probably
a lot of people here want to kill Frank
just as much as I do, and none of them will.
But it's early afternoon now and you're

watching the sunlight wandering
around among the ferns, picking out
one frond, then another, letting the darker
greens flicker into yellow as if in fact
the light was inventing this little dance

for you alone, giving you a reason
not to kill Frank, while reminding you
that men once believed the spores
of these very ferns could make
a person invisible, then disappear.

It's Not Just Trains

The ticket office was closing
when we arrived and were informed
our train had departed ahead of schedule.

"What do you mean?" I asked. "Trains
leave on time, or late, but never early."
"Such things happen," the agent replied,

"more often than you would think."
"Look around," he added,
"and pay attention. It's not just trains."

When I told my family of this unexpected
predicament, I was taken aback
by their lack of surprise. "Let's wander

a while through this pretty little town,"
my wife proposed, "and see what happens."
"Or else," said my son, "let's head off

into that dark woods beyond the tracks,
each alone and without our baggage,
and try to find our way out

before nightfall." He smiled, I thought,
at me in particular, as if he'd known
all along that would be the plan.

Parable of the Windows

If you want to get ahead, listen. *I did what*
I was told to is not a good answer. *It's the best*
I could come up with is even worse,

also ambiguous. What did you come up with—
that nonsense you showed me, or these excuses?
You think I'm pleased by ambiguity?

Well, so what if I am? I can afford it, which is why
I have all these windows. From the beginning
I knew this was going to be the story of my life,

even though I was born in a manger, cattle
all around, dirt all around, and for a while
I thought hard about being a savior,

I really did. But we already had too many,
so I decided on construction instead, got in
on the ground floor, and made it work,

and now I have all these windows—ten
in this office alone. And what
do you have? Excuses. And what do I have?

All these windows. Sometimes I look through
them and I forget the world, just staring into that
immaculate clarity. And you know what, my friend?

I could be up there. I could have my place at the table.
But looking makes me even happier than money,
and lets me love whatever I want to—like that

big horse of a cloud heading toward us
at this very moment. Like the darkness
that follows it. Like the light that comes after.

Testament

In my youth I wondered often about the past—
how it would change, and where it would end.
Now I can tell you many strange things
will never be revealed, and you
should be glad to know this.
When I vowed to discover the truth
I tried not to care about being believed.
I walked alone under the wild moon,
listened to the rain unfolding
its many propositions. Those were the days
of certainty and surmise. Thank you
for reading this far. Perhaps
you've found these pages by chance
and you're hoping for the wisdom
endings so often promise. Let me say:
Here or nowhere is the whole fact.
But assume nothing about this world,
neither its rules, nor any of its daily habits.
Nor how easily a man can throw
his life away. Or if,
in fact, I did. I won't excuse myself,
not now. The light that keeps the sky
in place is fading, but it's always fading.
Forget the past if you can. It's never over.
And then it is.

If I Knew What He Knew

I was standing on the rickety porch of my house
staring at the lawn, half-listening
to the radio where someone was explaining

it's a good idea to stay out of your own
backyard if you have trees there. Had dangerous
weather been predicted? Steve Jobs was sick,

and a man who once worked for him
was confessing: "I'd like to meet him in heaven
and say, 'Thank you.'" I wondered

how Steve Jobs, who wasn't yet in heaven,
might feel about that. I wondered if Steve Jobs
believed in heaven, and if inventing everything

he'd invented had changed his mind
on the subject, one way or the other.
"We should all be ashamed,"

an angry man on the next program insisted.
"Stupidity, stupidity, and more stupidity!"
And from the tone of his voice I believed

he was justified, that if I knew what he knew
I'd feel the same. The subject was history,
but it could have been heaven, and how angry

you were entitled to be if you'd been told when
or how you were going to die. And yet I understand
some people lie there calmly and whisper into the air.

The Hot Fives and Hot Sevens

"Now I know how a hamster feels,"
she said one morning, which made me wonder
if she saw herself as a pet in a cage, maybe
trapped, maybe loved. "I don't get it,"

I replied. And she told me if I had to ask
I'd never know, which was, I remembered,
what Louis Armstrong once said about jazz.
I was reluctant to mention this, although

early Armstrong seemed like a promising
subject—The Hot Fives and Hot Sevens—
some of her favorite records, great songs
she'd taught me how to listen to. So I said,

"Yes, I know what you mean." After which
nothing became poignant. And now,
years later, I still regret pretending to grasp
her point about the hamsters.

Was it exhaustion?—how they ran faster
and faster inside their little wheels.
Or indifference?—how carelessly
they often were treated. Or was it

deception?—beginning with all
the earlier evasions of death,
the goldfish and the turtles. Oh,
we knew what every child knows:

that they never vanish, that our mothers
and fathers whisked their bodies away
while we slept, as if they truly believed
they could spare us our grief.

I Was About to Go to Sleep

I'd seen him all day, sitting in his front yard,
looking straight ahead, so I figured
something was wrong, though not as wrong
as it turned out. But let me ask you first—
Does anyone who reads your newspaper
really need to know about this, just because
it happened? Doesn't it happen everywhere?
A man comes home from the war and can't
fit back into what used to be his life.
Then he can't imagine any life
that could be his. I won't say I've felt
that bad, but I understood how much
like a ghost he'd become. You sit there.
You see the desert, how far away it is.
You see the lawn and how impossible
it's become to mow it. You keep looking
straight ahead for a long time until
you don't see anything, because you're a ghost,
all hollowed out and waiting to vanish.
And then it's dark so you go inside the house
because that's where people go when it's dark.
And maybe you do what he did.
So I don't suppose I was telling the truth exactly
when I said I hadn't imagined how wrong
things had become. Why didn't I
walk over and speak to him that afternoon?
I could tell you I was afraid, and I was, but really
I had no words for the moment, not even one.
Yet I can hear myself speaking to him now.
"Is it like you're a ghost?" I ask, and he
replies, "Yes, sir, that's what it's like."
Leave that out, please, when you write your story.
Just say I saw him and was afraid.

Stuff

You lie down and everything falls out of your pockets,
coins first, then the little green halogen flashlight
and the blue pillbox, later your bulky ring of keys.
Where does that leave you? Unencumbered
and asleep, but it's a poor sleep with two pockets
of stuff to roll over on. Maybe some of these things
find their way into the troubles of your dreams,
and when you wake, you remember a man
with a ring of keys walking away, then turning back
and smiling. That's the end of it, so it's not a dream
that has much to tell you. After all, you were prodded
into it by everything scattered about on the bedspread.
And it was afternoon—time to let go of sleep,
fill your pockets, step outside. Forget what happened,
which now you're starting to see a little more of—
how he bent over you when he picked up
the keys, letting them slide across your cheek.

Almost, But Never

"This appealing legend," she explained
in the gallery while we studied the tapestry,
"does not correspond to historical facts."
I wanted to ask if knowing this changed
anything for her, or if my question,
which I didn't ask, was beside the point.

In the tapestry there were many oaks,
and many hunters on horseback among
these oaks, brandishing long spears as their dogs
raced gracefully beside them. And yet it appeared
nothing was moving. Was that the idea—
they were all helplessly trapped in the moment?

But she was recounting the legend,
most of which I'd missed. A heart was involved,
or a hart, or both, and a beautiful woman
tied to an oak, and two kings, each one
powerful and jealous. I wanted to ask
if this wasn't in fact very close to King Arthur,

but so what if it was, I didn't care, I just felt like
saying something so she'd have to look at me,
our tour guide, who was slim and lovely
and spoke with a light Italian accent, and who,
when pointing out some detail, almost, but never,
touched the surface of what we were trying to see.

A Plain White Envelope

I let the envelope fall to the floor unopened,
and yes, it felt falsely dramatic, even if she
was no longer there to point that out. Let me
go back and set the scene: mid-afternoon,

too early for a drink but a reasonable time
to start thinking about one. In the kitchen:
a plain white envelope propped against
the salt shaker. I won't pretend to be surprised.

I watch it for a while, then flick it onto the floor
and nudge it under that ugly bird's-eye
maple cabinet of mismatched dishes, way back
where it might easily be overlooked when the house

is cleaned. Some day you may find yourself
living here for a month in the summer,
and one afternoon the clear light from the water,
which I remember so fondly, will touch an edge

of that envelope as you sit by the window. Of course
you'll kneel down to pull it out. And yet
you hesitate. Why not open it?
It's as much yours as anyone's now.

The Truth of the Cookie

After we'd finished all of General Tsao's chicken
I cracked my fortune cookie open and read,
Don't romanticize that which is distant.
"Does this sound like a fortune?" I complained
to my wife. "It sounds," she replied,

"like good advice, especially for you."
That's what irked me—the personal gist of it.
Certainly this was no chance occurrence.
Someone out in the kitchen had been told:
See that guy with the gray moustache?

Make sure he gets this cookie. "It's uncanny,"
I said. "Who could know how often
I'm tempted to romanticize the past?"
"Nobody," she answered. "Lots of people
feel that way, which is the truth of the cookie."

A good point—yes, but not the whole truth.
"Real fortunes are always about the future,"
I insisted. "Tell me what you got." "*Someone
will invite you to a Karaoke party.*" "See!—
it's the future. That's the essence of the genre."

"You aren't leaving enough of a tip,"
she whispered. But couldn't she tell
my soul had been touched and bruised?
"Next time," I said, "let's go to the Indian place.
Let's not meddle with the supernatural."

"Oh!" she exclaimed, "Isn't that a great line
for a cookie? Soon you will *meddle
with the supernatural.*" "No," I replied,

though all the way home I kept wondering
what I'd ever wanted the past to be.

The System

The system looks perfect to those who understand it.
The poor get little because they need a lot,
while the rich, who don't, get more.

So the poor spend all day lying around
as though they were rich, but that's not
what they're thinking. As for me,

if I were rich I'd devote my life
to sleep, which I'd explain is the way
to stave off death. And if anyone

were to tell me how stupid this idea
really is, I'd reply, *Of course
that's just your opinion, which I don't share*

because I'm rich. And if I were poor?
I'd dedicate myself even harder
to the intricacies of this system,

its pathways and vistas, its detours
and dead ends, and all of the shadowy corners
where sometimes the rich appear

to ask for my trust. Believe us, they whisper.
What you can't have you don't need.
What you were never given you can never lose.

Another Scenario

"Harry," someone tells me, "for that kind of money
bad things happen to people." Which was how
I made the connection between money and nothing,

and saw the street after midnight where I'd be
outnumbered and alone under the bridge.
But there's always another scenario,

and in it the plot will be treating me
quite differently. I might be standing with you
by a lake at twilight. I might hear

some kind of bird singing, and feel lucky.
"We don't like to say much," others told me,
"because we don't want to lose our lives."

That made sense, I respected that, and I believe
the scenario wanted me to feel the same,
meaning afraid, meaning awestruck

at all the bad things that can happen
to people, then uncertain if the opposite
could have been arranged instead—

like walking out into the sun without even
a penny in my pocket, wondering
where you might be. I'm back in the city

right now, quite well-dressed in fact, and waiting
for a train. "Harry," the man behind me says,
"don't stand too close to the edge. At least not yet."

2

Restoration

I   The Weight

This weight on my chest,
this sullen sadness—tell me, Doctor,
how I can lift it up and set it down.
I want to be reassured by a fact,
by some measurable fever. To say:
That's why I need to sleep.

               And no—
this isn't what I felt last week.
And yes, I'd like to have the past back.
But what would I do with it except what I did?
If I walk out into the garden, Doctor,
will loveliness help?

               This sadness,
this weight on your chest—
why shouldn't it hurt? Perhaps
it will pass.

             Perhaps you will find
some necessary task, one you may believe
you can't undertake. Don't think about it.
Happiness isn't any easier to explain.

2   If I'm Watching You Down in the Garden

A drawing of a tree shows not a tree
but a tree being looked at.
                    —John Berger

Maybe nothing's only itself when we're looking.
Not this silver maple. Not you.
The wind arrives, turning the leaves over.
The crow chooses a branch
just for a moment. If I'm watching you

down in the garden, are you more yourself
because you don't know that I'm looking?
Then you glance up at the bird.
At least that's the way I'm arranging it,
and I understand the tree is a prop

and the crow could be a hawk
if I needed a hawk, but you,
who have been the figure in this landscape,
are walking inside now, picking up
the phone, dialing a number.

What do I want you to tell me?
What would you say if it were yours to say?

3   At About This Hour

Everyone except Julie was dancing badly,
and I was sitting there watching with Tom
who had a broken ankle for his excuse.
Mary would be leaving in the morning.
I didn't know how she felt. Or for that matter
how I might be feeling from one moment
to the next—sometimes happier
than I'd expect, walking down a path
bordered by pines, sometimes bleaker
than I could attach any reason to.
Then people decided they'd go swimming,
and I headed back to my room. The air
was close and fragrant: no stars,
a little lightning far off to the east
that hadn't a chance of reaching us. Things
would settle down. I could hear the traffic
on the Northway as I heard it every night
unless I forgot to listen. "It's better
if you go to Italy and do something there,"
Carolina had said at dinner. At another table
Andy exclaimed: "They gave me a hat—
I have the hat to this day!" People laughed.
And then someone whose name I can't recall
asked someone else: "Why do you want
to remember the past?" And I thought:
Do we have a choice? Doesn't it just return?
In a few days I'd be gone, but maybe
one night at about this hour I'd stop
and think back. Would I wish
I were here?—the party over, the lightning
fading away beyond the mountains,
and on the road all those travelers—
so many destinations ahead of them,
so many chances of arriving unharmed.

4   My Father's Question

Is there anything you want to know?
my father once asked me. I can't picture
the scene. Were we out on the lawn?
Was a baseball involved? No, I said,

taken by surprise. And he turned away,
embarrassed and relieved.
But he must have understood
that wasn't the right question, not even close.

How many questions aren't even close?
How many times are we given a moment
that could be important, then isn't?
Caverns and crevices, dark places
where all the secrets are squirreled away—

this is the stuff of the books I read as a boy,
the crimes that were solved
by good friends who never grew older.
In the end you did what you could on your own.

We kept to ourselves, my father and I.
We learned the strategies
of letting things be. But there we were
out on the lawn that afternoon,
a blaze of heat all around us.

What would you have told me
if I'd been able to ask?
Look—even now
I'm only pretending to speak to you.

5   The Slamming of a Door Downstairs

jars me from my sleep and when I open
my eyes there are the little white stars
of consciousness dancing before me

until the room slides back into focus.
I'd been wondering: Why can't I
love the world as I wish to? What keeps

falling between us like the gray scarf
of a man who refuses to stop mourning?
There's the sky, the branches of trees

waving their green flags in the wind.
The sun falls evenly on the grass
and has nothing to tell me.

Or it does and I don't know
how to listen. When a hand
unclenches inside my heart

for a while I'm myself, and I can see
the world isn't asking for my love.
It will continue laboring

under its own weight just like
the rest of us. Then we're only
ourselves. We're all we have left.

There's the sky, paler than yesterday,
like some singleness of purpose—
like anything, really, I might want it to be.

6   Heroic

"People who plan their own memorial services,"
my friend was saying, "don't get the point of death."
There'd been songs and prayers and ecumenical
readings. Then one of the children played the trumpet,
and the brother spoke too long without being funny
or sad. Now we were headed to the reception
to be sincere about how much he'd have appreciated it.

But I liked thinking you could say of someone,
He didn't get the point of death, and make it sound
like a brave refusal. As we walked up the hill
on that stubbornly beautiful day, I liked that idea
a lot more than hearing about people battling their illnesses
when all they're really doing is lying there with a chemo drip

in their arms, then stumbling off to throw up. I know,
I know it's only a figure of speech, a way of granting
courage to those whose bodies can't manage it,
but what I want is the strapping on of bright armor,
the hefting of great swords, then striding out
into the blinding plain, massed armies on either side.
Sure, the odds are against us. In fact, we're doomed,

which is why the clarity of standing here
has become important—not the battle itself, but these
few minutes of stillness, the ocean in the distance
brandishing its light, and the seabirds inscribing
their invisible maps across the field of the sky,
and the colorful flags of our armies testing the wind.

7   So Much More Mournful Than Before

This morning, remembering the end
of an unpleasant dream, it seemed important
to think about Edgar Allan Poe.
Was he really afraid of being buried alive?
Or had he figured out exactly
how nervous he could make us?

He was always burying something
that wouldn't stay buried, or walling up
what he'd have to face when that wall
got torn down. But maybe Poe

was only a rhyme at the edge of my dream,
the way one thing connects to another
until it floats away: rows of beans,
flowers of evil. Now it's evening
and I'm listening to Joe Lovano playing
a song called "I Have the Room Above Her,"

which feels sweet enough until the title
reminds me of Roderick Usher listening
to his sister waking up in the tomb.
Oh, it was all preventable, everything they did,

but it felt inevitable, which is how
people's lives unfold in a well-made story.
We see what they don't, and sometimes
we think of ourselves.
What should I be afraid of?

Perhaps that dream was trying to keep
the answer hidden, and now
it's gone, so I can't explain why I thought of Poe
and all his extravagant disguises,

or why, as the song ends, Lovano sounds
so much more mournful than before.

8   Little Bird

One cloud was following another
across a blue and passionless sky.
It was the middle of summer, far enough
from December for a man to feel indifferent
to the memories of cold, not yet close
enough to autumn to be caught up
in all its folderol about death.
Neither cloud looked like a whale
or a weasel, or any kind of fanciful beast.
All morning I'd wanted
to sit my life down in a comfortable chair,
tell it to stop worrying, and walk away as if
I were somebody else, somebody without a house
or a family or a job, but somebody who might
soon feel with a pang precisely the absence
of everything I had. A cool breeze lifted
the curtains in the room where I was sitting.
A bird was singing, nearby
but out of sight. Had it been singing for long?
Far off there were mountains, but I didn't
want to go there. Nor did I yearn
to be standing by a lake, or walking
beside the tumult of the sea.
The little bird kept repeating its song.
I filled a glass and watched the water tremble.

9   Restoration

Making something the way it was—
what could I have been thinking
months ago when I wrote that line
in my notebook? I liked the way the words
fit together, and perhaps it was well below zero
that morning, the furnace acting up again,
and I was feeling particularly mortal,
just a few weeks after the operation on my spine.
Yet how easily an occasion explains more
than it should, and how risky, how exacting
is the work of the surgeon, and of the great restorers—

each layer of varnish slowly disappearing
from another grimy masterpiece until
the luminous colors must be as they were
when Turner or Piero stepped back and nodded
in satisfaction. *This is what they saw*
is what I want to believe—the way the world
once was, even if no one can swear to it,

a thousand smart guesses having turned
into choices—what to remove, what to leave
undisturbed. That tiny smudge of a dog
sleeping far from the cross was there
from the beginning. But the vivid plume of smoke
above the crippled ship? Or the precise stare

of that angel? Should her eyes be so cold?
Should she really be looking at me
with such casual indifference, as if hundreds
of years ago I'd never have begged: *Come down,*
show me your face, make me whole again.

10   Last Evening

for Julie and Ryan

It's nearing the end of June 20,
the day after a day of storms.
We felt we deserved this beauty.

Now I'm watching evening slowly
settle in: my friends wandering
across the lawn, layers of clouds

back-lit as if they were proving
something tender in a movie,
everything setting the scene

for the moment that follows.
What does nature teach us?
Nature lets us decide.

Swallows dash through the twilight
and I don't think about
what they might mean. Or I didn't

just then. They swooped in and were gone.
It got dark. One more bird sang
briefly off in the trees, and I felt

grateful to be standing there, letting
the moment pass through me
as if that was all that had to happen.

3

The Major Subjects

Death is easier
than love. And true feeling, as someone said,
leaves no memory. Or else
memory replaces the past, which we know
never promised to be true.

Consider the sea cucumber:
when attacked it divides, sacrificing half
so that half
won't get eaten. Can the part left undevoured
figure out what to do?

The natural world is always instructive,
mysterious as well, but often
hard to praise. Love
is also difficult—the way it slides
into so many other subjects,

like murder, deceit,
and the moon. As my mother used to say
about anything
we couldn't find: If it had been
a snake it would have bitten you.

Fellow poets, we must
learn again to copy from nature,
see for ourselves
how steadfastly even its beauty
refuses to care or console.

The Mortality of Books

Dampness and sunshine
are equally fatal. Jackets fade, mildew
gathers. Whatever you wipe away
will surely return. But now, sliding

that last book back in place, you see
the afternoon you first held it in your hands—
light through the lace
of the trees, and at home the sheen of the table

where it lay, proclaiming its beauty,
later the shelf where it remained, exiled
and unread, as if its purpose had always been
to remind you of the brevity of what's new.

You didn't think about it then.
The sun was out, the books were shining
in their displays along the avenue,
and you were certain you'd fallen in love.

Remember that day?
Everything was a bargain. And mortality?
That was an idea,
one word among the others.

A Couple of Disasters and a Lot of Landscape

for Carin Clevidence

First the explosion of the fireworks factory,
later the hurricane. First a tree full
of tiny American flags, then no trees at all.

A long story needs at least one disaster
to show us how people act when they're caught
off-guard, whereas the landscape
in between is a good place for detail

and second thoughts. *Yes*, she decides,
that's why I never answered his letter,
or went out that night in the rain.
The writer knows the trick is always
balance. Too much thinking is worse

than too much action, except for Proust.
And many other equally persuasive exceptions,
which remind us the best advice exists
to be disregarded once it's understood.

Aftermath is for the difficult truths.
Is that where our house used to be?
the wife asks, hoping the answer isn't
what she can see so clearly—
many pages torn from a book, and a spoon,

the umbrella no one ever used, two letters
still unopened—all the secrets of debris,
and everything they mean if they mean
anything beyond the strangeness of what survives.

Last Day on Earth

If it's the title of a movie you expect
everything to become important—a kiss,
a shrug, a glass of wine, a walk with the dog.

But if the day is real, life is only
as significant as yesterday—the kiss
hurried, the shrug forgotten, and now,

on the path by the river, you don't notice
the sky darkening beyond the pines because
you're imagining what you'll say at dinner,

swirling the wine in your glass.
You don't notice the birds growing silent
or the cold towers of clouds moving in,

because you're explaining how lovely
and cool it was in the woods. And the dog
had stopped limping!—she seemed

her old self again, sniffing the air and alert,
the way dogs are to whatever we can't see.
And I was happy, you hear yourself saying,

because it felt as if I'd been allowed
to choose my last day on earth,
and this was the one I chose.

The Sirens

After a while we got tired of singing.
One morning out on the rocks
with not a ship in sight, we all felt it—

a certain weariness, a malaise,
if you will. We felt it together,
sympathy having become

one of the finer aspects
of our nature. We've drifted apart
since those days, yet we're happy

being remembered as impossible
to resist. The legends used to claim
we knew the future as well—*all things*

which shall be hereafter upon the earth,
as our song put it. Everyone only assumed
we were beautiful. But we were, and are,

though not unlike so many other
women now, those who promise much less,
but let you live. It was a relief

to give up our powers willingly.
That didn't happen often in our world,
where the gods went on amusing themselves

with their meddling, and the hero
plowed ahead, lashed to the mast,
dying to be tempted. Did we enjoy the clamor

of shipwreck? The cries of the disillusioned?
It was our job, our particular talent.
We weren't supposed to want anything else.

After the Fall of the House of Usher

for Michael Bell

Sometimes I think I made it all up,
that if I returned I'd be told
there'd never been a house beside that tarn—
who would build anything in such a place?

But I'm not asking you to believe
a tale you probably never thought was true,
at least in the way we used to think
about the truth, meaning that it happened.
I'm just looking back, since I can see

my own death not so far away, and I worry
that what I wrote feels too *excited,*
too eager to create *effects,* though I like effects.
Beauty and terror—how companionable
they were in those days! But at the end

I really was afraid. I know you want
to hear why we put her in the tomb,
then screwed the lid of the coffin down.
Couldn't we have left the poor woman
alone in her bed, let her wake up,
if she was going to, as if from a dream?

What can I say?—it didn't occur to me
at the time. I'm not a doctor, just a friend
and a narrator. She had physicians, I specifically
mention that fact, and I saw her
only once, briefly, far across the room.

Of course Usher knew. He could hear her

rustling around in the dark, figuring out
where she was. And then he called *me* mad—
*"Madman, I tell you that now she stands
without the door!"* That's close enough

to what he actually said, and I remember
feeling unnerved and taken aback.
Why was he yelling at *me?* Then the wind
tore everything apart, and we saw her.

Yes, I've changed a few of the details,
but it's been so long I couldn't say which ones.
I must have thought that another touch
of atmosphere might help convey
the way it was. Yet how ordinary
so many strange things turn out to be,

like dreams that end up disappointing us
by making sense. Look,
I wasn't there to save anyone.
I just tried to be his friend.

The Beginning of Philosophy

for Christian Thorne

We've reached that time of night when repetition
starts looking like the best kind of argument,
so I continue to insist it was *wrong*—meaning
what they did in the remake of *Cat People.*
No, my friend replies, just different,

more attentive to the worries of the moment.
But I prefer the old worries: the snapping
of branches, footsteps in the fog, then the hiss
of the bus that wasn't a panther, but will be.
Why do we need to see so much?

To know what we're afraid of, he says,
and since it's late I tell him this is like
the beginning of philosophy all over again—
one proposition, then another,
and after a few thousand years we're back

to what's true, or only seems to be:
flickering light on the wall, that confusion
of shadows. How still the room becomes.
A little rain touches the windows,
and both of us mention other movies

in which not even love can repair the past.
Then the snow mixes in. And yet, my friend
says, by morning all this could change.
No nagging doubts, no secret afflictions—
as if the light had burned them away.

And a man might find himself
wondering about the sky instead.
Why is it so blue? Why do we feel
different when the sun grabs hold of us?
Why do we need to be sure of anything?

Ophelia at Home

I didn't drown. All those eloquent
reports were a misunderstanding,
and that jumping into the grave
was added later, the way things often are
to make a scene more exciting.
Horatio got it to work as a play,
though I never thought it made much sense.
But I knew that turning up alive
would be a problem for him.
And in fact I preferred to remain drowned,
let my mad songs be my last words.
I moved far away from Denmark,
married, had children. And now I've lived
a long time with someone else's name,
long enough to see how the past changes
depending on what kind of king
is in power, what kind of affection
in fashion. No one, in my opinion,
needs to know if we slept together,
or when he actually went mad,
or how I was rescued from that stream
and got better. I'll just say
he was wrong about women
never being both beautiful and honest.
Not that he meant it. He was always
too fond of words, and maybe a little afraid
of being alone. Or of being with me.
But I don't intend to make the story
any clearer. He said he loved me,
and I believed him
even when he said he didn't.
I was a girl, after all.
I wanted things to work out.

Original Sin

That was one idea my mother
always disliked. She preferred her god
to be reasonable, like Emerson or Thoreau
without their stranger moments.
Even the Old Testament God's
sudden angers and twisted ways
of getting what he wanted she'd accept
as metaphor. But original sin
was different. Plus no one agreed
if it was personal, meaning
all Adam's fault, or else some kind
of temporary absence of the holy,
which was Adam's fault as well.
In any case, it made no sense
that we'd need to be saved before
we'd even had the chance
to be wrong. Yes, eventually everyone
falls into error, but when my sister and I
were babies she could see we were perfect,
as we opened our eyes and gazed up at her
with what she took for granted as love,
long before either of us knew the word
and what damage it could cause.

When Time Slows Down

Now I'm lying in a narrow hospital bed,
waiting for the first tests to come back,
raising the cup of apple juice to my lips,
then setting it back on the table
very carefully. I've been watching
a large round clock, so much like

the clocks in the schoolrooms
of childhood, where the big hand *clicked*
loudly as another minute was forced into place.
Was it fourth grade or fifth?
And I'm still waiting, unable to recall

why I've been sent to the principal's office,
one future after another sweeping past me
as I stare at his door until
finally I'm there and he says,
So let's hear your side of the story.
Whatever I did is gone, but not

the certainty of time slowing down,
or the desire to rise from my chair
—or now this bed—and float
outside, unfettered
and careless, beyond judgment or change.

When Mythology Was the Truth

after Wallace Stevens

If we had lived in a time when mythology
was the truth, what tales
would have satisfied us? Could the poem

take the place of the gods in Connecticut
or Vermont? The image tries hard to collect
a mountain and its streams, and the poem

stands atop the summit, gazing
in all directions. Everywhere
prospects present themselves.

So the cloud floats into place,
the treetops sway, and alone in its plot
the mulberry deepens its shade,

while the weeds in the gulley are like armies,
no—like water under the ship
that carries the hero home.

I Was Just Wondering

If the universe keeps expanding,
where is it going, and what
was here before? Don't tell me nothing.
If God made us, and was pleased,

why did he decide to add
the Japanese beetle? Or the deer tick?
Or any kind of disease that steals your mind?
When did that look like a good idea?

And don't tell me there's a plan
but we're not supposed to know
how it works. What's the point of guessing?
Why should a turtle live a hundred years

but not a dog, specifically my dog?
Why do we sometimes need each other,
and sometimes not? Don't tell me
more happiness wouldn't make as good a story.

And if we say we love what fades
because it fades, how will we feel
when we start to forget?
Don't tell me we shouldn't be afraid.

Nothing

Why not believe death is also nothing?
—Dean Young

Sometimes nothing's a glass
waiting to be filled, and sometimes

it's sleep without dreams, a blank slate
no one gets to leave a message on,

that sheet of water boys skip stones across
to watch them vanish. And sometimes

nothing's only a word that can hide
what it means inside what it means.

But when I've seen death it's looked
like betrayal, like life taking back

what it promised, slowly picking
our friends apart until nothing

must feel like an answer, and death
slips into the room pretending to care.

Did it brush by me just now,
did it mean to touch my hand?

What I Should Tell You More Often

for Judy

If I couldn't hear your voice no other voice
would suffice. If I couldn't listen
to your breath as you sleep, how would I
know I was still breathing?

How could I open my eyes
to receive the day? If we forget
the same story, what time takes from us

it takes from us both. But if you
weren't to return to this room,
why would I draw the curtains to divide
one darkness from another?

Why would I need to make that distinction?
What we see together each morning
without surprise, how quickly would it vanish?—

those stones in the garden adding up to a wall,
and the grass that has learned
where it must end, and the flowers whose names
only you have tried to teach me.

4

A Cup of Water Turns into a Rose

I

On the radio a choir was singing
"I want to be a crocus"
in a mournful British accent.

One of the three men who wasn't me
expressed disapproval. He seemed to know
the composer's work, may in fact have had

some personal connection, which couldn't
have been a happy one. I followed them
into another room where soon enough

I understood their conversation
wasn't meant to include me, and so,
feeling like an intruder, as seems often

the case at the end of a dream, I woke up.

*

There'd been a long unwinding narrative,
perfectly coherent until all of it was lost

when the music began and I noticed
the radio—shiny and black, with huge dials,
like nothing I'd ever owned, maybe

something out of the Second World War,
or a movie about it: anxious men bent forward

around what now had turned into the forbidden

short-wave equipment—static that opened up
to a voice declaring in code the time of a landing
on some important beach nearby. Within hours

everybody's lives would change,
and the excitement on their faces
was illuminated by the glowing of the dial.

*

I'd seen other versions of that story,
and could predict who wouldn't survive,
cradled in the arms of his best friend—

the selfless bravery of his dying,
the way he'd slowly close his eyes
after his choked but eloquent final words.

Had he made a last request—a sweetheart
back home who needed to be told,
a father who'd never understood?

Was a letter involved, a medal, a ring?
No doubt such deaths occurred, such tokens
were passed from hand to hand.

*

As seems often the case these days
I woke up troubled by the purposeless
weight on my chest. I knew that later

that morning a few pills would help,
a walk with the dogs, a way to choose
what I could expect to accomplish, a way

to calculate the lengthening of the day,
to see it moving toward dusk, then evening.
But now the birds were beginning

their chorus, and the folds of sleep
unhanded me. No, Doctor, I don't
want to die, if that's what you're asking.

I'd just rather not wake up.

✹

For it might be at first thought, wrote John Ruskin,
whom I must admit I've hardly read,
that the whole kingdom of imagination

was one of deception also. Not so. Let's admire
that brave stab at brevity—*Not so*—even if
it's followed by a colon, and the reader's

certainty that Ruskin will never settle for
a single word when two or three present themselves.
Therefore the imagination is a summoning

of things absent or impossible.
And the force of it lies
in the knowledge of their actual absence

or impossibility at the moment
of their apparent presence . . . We invent
and observe what does not exist,

and at that moment we are pleased to see
what we have made, and how it cannot be real.

✶

Their code was never broken. The invasion
would succeed, but not without cost. Later
the father bows his head, and turns away,

the girl tries hard not to cry—an expression
of resignation, then of pride, crossing her face.
She'll refold the letter and show it to no one.

"Do you think that's from *They Were Expendable*,"
I ask a man who looks like he might know.
"It's not," he replies. We're standing on a road

among tall white pines, and a pleasant breeze
has found us there, so I say, "It helps—
nature—at times, though it doesn't mean to."

"At times," he says, "the impossible
looks like it's on our side
until it isn't." He shakes his head.

"I knew Ruskin—he was a jerk." I nod,
as if I'd known him too, and felt the same.

2

Yun-Fei makes a picture called
"Mistaking Each Other for Ghosts."
"Which ones are the ghosts?"
I ask, and he smiles.

"Ghosts are good to mix with other things,"
he tells me. "See, the people
are in their own world, and the ghosts
surround them. But it's each other

the people don't recognize."

*

And sometimes a strange creature appears,
not exactly a ghost but part of the space
from which the ghost emerges, and again
people fail to see it, sensing only
this wind, how comforting it is, or how bitter.
There was something else I wanted to tell you.

*

We're standing on that road bordered by pines,
and I notice the man is very well-dressed
and I'm not. "Earlier," he finally says,

"you must have been dreaming
of Benjamin Britten's wretched setting
of 'I want to be a crocus.'" "Yes," I answer,

"how acute you are! I'd started thinking
it was Vaughan Williams, but of course
that could never be the case."

☼

It's in the nature of the moment
to remind us of its vanishing,
I tell my friend Ralph, who says
he doesn't feel that way at all.

You're lucky, I reply, and he shrugs.
He tells me he's still not sleeping well.
But what can you do?
Lunch? he asks. The usual?

On vacations I'd often count the days
that remained, and in this way pleasure
became diminishment, the present always
slipping away, the future staking its claims.

If I'd not wanted to write poems,
I tell myself, I would have been
a happier person, though of course
I have no reason to believe this.

☼

"Write about love," my wife suggests,
"a long poem about aging and love,
with at least three geographical locations,
two or more references to the natural world,

two or more references to politics and history,
and no dreams or ghosts. Or write
a poem entitled 'Plant Life.' Or else:
'Visiting the Museum with My Daughter.'
But start with the one about love."

＊

The ghosts come out at night.
The dead can still dance. Yet where
they once were, Yun-Fei explains,
they can live no longer, since the dam
has destroyed their empire, the lake

covered the world they drifted through,
not always hidden from the living.
Yet they dance. They rise
out of the water. They dance in the air
above their drowned city.

3

Did you make your sister cry?

Yes, I did.

Did you tell her there were snakes under her bed?

Yes.

Well go say you're sorry,
that you made it all up, that there's nothing
in her room to be frightened of.

And in her closet?

And in her closet too.

＊

Each summer when I was growing up there were cows
in that stony pasture on the way to our cottage
by the lake in New Hampshire.

If they were lying down as we drove by
my mother would say it was a sign of rain,
no matter how cloudless the sky

arching over us, assuring us
that everything would be like this,
that nothing, no matter what I wanted,

would ever really change.

Music drifted out of the elegant old house,
across the lawn, down to the sea—
Tommy Dorsey, perhaps, or Glenn Miller.

Were we back in the war?
The evening seemed like a gift
from a god who'd decided it was time

we faced more than the usual uncertainties.
So we wandered. We were meant to be
aimless and worried, but also unaffected by life

beyond this moment. "It's like a dream,"
Wendy said. "A dream without
a secret," Anne replied. "No, it's like

a movie," Jonathan insisted, "the one
where they're on a ship but unable
to remember their destination, unaware

that they're already dead." We tried
to think of the title. No one offered
to go inside and find out. "Not oblivion,"

said Mark, "but the moment before."
Not death but a long party on a dark night,
all of us out on the lawn as if fireworks

had been promised, which explained why
every so often we looked up at the sky.

"That's all very pretty," says the man
who disliked Ruskin, "all very *evocative*,
if you know what I mean, very *sad*,

but not really sad in the way we actually feel,
languid, rather, as if that was all we had
the energy to feel. And in addition," he adds,

"it's more like a poem by somebody else,
so maybe you should call it that: 'A Poem
by Somebody Else Interrupts My Poem.'

Or else: 'Visiting the Museum with My Daughter,'
since it would work much better as a painting—
by someone very good, of course,

someone who knew how to paint the sky."

*

We could chance upon it, my daughter and I,
that landscape where people once were
but from which they seem to have been removed,

as if the artist came to trust the light in the grass,
the way it kept pointing to what wasn't there,
perhaps a cross, perhaps a child.

*

In the dream that repeated itself
for months after my mother's death,
we're in a room that looks like home,

summer light in the picture window,
and she's in her chair, though I know
she shouldn't be. And yet she hasn't died—

that was a mistake, my mistake.
Light fills the window until it's impossible
to look outside. You were sick, I say,

but now you're better. You went away,
but now you're back. How foolish I was
to miss you for no reason.

4

When I was a boy I liked things
left up in the air, the unexplained, the strange
but true, like the story of the German U-boat

in the closing days of the war—how desperately
the crew attempts to escape the American
depth-charges, cutting the engines, letting

themselves sink deeper and deeper, sweating
and holding their breaths until *somewhere*
a pounding begins, like a man outside

under the impossible weight of the sea
declaring, *This is where we are!*
The war's all but over, Hitler's dead,

the captain surrenders, and a year later
as the boat's being dismantled for scrap,
the skeleton of a worker is discovered

sealed up between the inner
and outer hulls, a large wrench
still clutched in what's left of his hand.

*

And sometimes the plot hinged on a lighthouse
and a cave. A motorboat idling in the bay,
because they like to come ashore at night.

Money concealed in a trunk.
Or a letter someone's life
depends upon. Fog settling in.

Then not far from where the boy's
been hiding: a crunch of pebbles,
the sound a man makes who's trying

very hard not to give himself away.
The point was never who should be trusted,
the point was always how much

you could do on your own.

*

One afternoon I overheard my daughter
talking on her red and white toy telephone.

"When you get old," she said, "you die.
But sometimes even little children die."
She wasn't sad, I thought, or even worried,

but whoever was listening had to be told
that story over and over,
and she kept on explaining.

*

And later in the distance: the muffled
noise of traffic, all of the ordinary
comings and goings, the way it is
at every moment that's important.

✲

The peonies on my desk struggle to open,
sticky beads like sweat on the tight buds.
If I could get close enough I'd hear

some sound inside, straining. All afternoon
I drifted in and out of sleep, whatever story
was in my mind sliding off course

then swerving back. One man hands another
a folded piece of paper. Someone turns
a radio on—distant music, then a voice.

Meanwhile the sky began to clear,
such brightness suggesting sleep was wrong,
I'd get nothing from it. The fist

of a bud sprung into petals is almost
a hand, my father's hand opening,
then setting itself down. I can see it's hard.

As we stood around his bed we said it:
what hard work dying seems to be.

✲

In a dream even a pebble is a clue,
or can become one, the way a cup of water
turns into a rose, and the rose
into a ring, then a letter, then a face
in a mirror, and soon I'm waiting

for a friend in an old train station,
and a man steps out of the crowd and says,
"Where do you think you're going with that?"
"With what?" I ask. "With that thing," he says,
"that thing you have in your hand."

5

"In my vision, in the vanity of my art,"
I imagine Prospero confessing
to the audience, still clutching his staff,
"in that pretty spectacle I made for the children,

you may not have noticed I left out winter.
That was a sweet illusion—leaping
from harvest to springtime—not true,
of course, which doesn't make it wrong,

just impossible. You could say
I was close enough to death
that I didn't want to think about it,
but if you were paying attention

you knew death was always on my mind.
And how to give away what I still had
to give away. Now imagine me
in Milan, crossing a busy street,

too much like everyone else.
Not that old man. Not that one either.
Keep watching. Then let me go."

*

It is necessary to our rank
as spiritual creatures, Ruskin continues,
that we should be able to invent and to behold
what is not. And to grieve for it,

as Prospero grieved for the limitations
of his art. And the actor playing him for his.

✳

"Oh, Ruskin again," sighs the man on the road.
"Why not stick to Shakespeare? Or give
Emerson a try: *Memory is a presumption*

of a possession of the future. Too wordy?
Then what about: *There is no other world;*
here or nowhere is the whole fact.

On the other hand, don't be so serious all the time.
Didn't your mother tell you that? Didn't your sister
encourage you to take up golf?" We walk a while

down the shady lane. "Now you sound too much
like me," I tell him. "You're supposed to be
someone else." But he isn't paying attention.

"Or how about this," he declares. *"All illusions*
look real, or they wouldn't be illusions, would they?
Seek out the metaphysical where it really lives—

Dracula vs. Frankenstein, 1971,
one of the worst movies ever made. Look it up.
I'm not going to tell you who wins."

✳

"What happens to you when you die?"
my daughter asked her mother, who told her,
being careful, that some people think
you go to heaven. "Yes," she said,
"but what do the others think?"

*

What does the past intend to show us now?
Pines, oaks. A fly on a screen.
September's weeds and vines.

High in the maples the first few streaks
of color might even suggest the worry
a child feels at the end of summer—

how we can't help looking back so quickly,
wanting what we had, even if when we had it
we wanted something else.

*

Nothing more to see: night
pressed against the windows.
But on the porch my mother can hear
birds in the woods still singing.
So it isn't night completely.

Let the children stay out a little longer,
she thinks, listening to them

as they leap from their hiding places
and run off before they've been touched.

On such an evening she must have played
this game herself. What was it called?
Or perhaps it never had a name.

6

"How are you feeling right now?" my companion
inquires. "Mornings are the worst,"
I tell him. "Of course they are," he says.

"You could try to be more sympathetic."
"Be sympathetic to yourself," he replies,
"that's not why I'm here. And by the way,

you should learn the actual names
of trees. You're always talking about trees,
and birds, and behind them the sky. Moreover,

pines don't count." "And exactly why
are you here?" I say. "Because you asked,
because you need me, because I don't
have anything better to do."

*

"I was bored," the scientist said, "and I began
thinking—what happens to a memory
when you remember it? Can you play with it?

Can you change it? And so it appears
that each time we call up the past
the details reshuffle. Each time

without our trying to, the past is revised,
and since the mind doesn't file away its drafts,
what once was there is gone, leaving us

only the latest images of the truth."

*

As for instance, walking a little way down
a path in a forest, wanting life to change,
even if it has. Or any day when the future sweeps
across the landscape you happen to be passing.
A moment earlier and you'd have missed it.

As for instance, a dream like the real course
of a dream—but with an idea running all through it.
Two people unaware they await the same occurrence.
The page of a book picked up, by chance, in the street.
You can't get it right. You can't leave it the way it is.

*

A few notes from a piano
and night descends. Later the wind
moves east, shaking the loose doors of houses
all along the coast. In one of those
frail cabins we were sleeping.

Although that was years ago

I can hear the seabirds crying, and the rush
of the wind—how it woke us as we dreamt
fitfully, like the other travelers.
How we both thought we'd left something undone

until we remembered where we were.

When I was a boy I tried to believe in heaven,
to accept the process of punishment
and reward, which led to the idea that nothing
would ever truly be lost. I wasn't successful.

I saved things instead: coins and postcards,
coasters and stamps, matchbooks from restaurants
my parents had gone to, clippings describing
my favorite TV shows: *The Twilight Zone,*
One Step Beyond. I can still feel

the chill when I heard about that submarine,
and the man trapped inside, and the wrench
in his hand—then the narrator
quietly adding, "Explain it
I cannot. But wouldn't it be terrifying

if everything was known?"

Then there's a day that looks so perfectly
composed I can't help but hear my mother
saying, *For heaven's sake, go outside,*

as if I were still the boy who preferred
rainy afternoons. But I do what she tells me,
take the dogs and head up Stone Hill,

where all along the stubbly fields
the maples are poised and extravagant,

coming into their own together.

A few leaves float away from their branches
to remind me how beauty loves death.
Then the sun slips behind a cloud,

and the luminous trees withdraw
into the general prospect, suggesting
I might want to think harder. But I've no desire

to make the landscape speak for me.
*How do we know when we've felt enough
of anything?* my mother might have asked,

although that doesn't sound like her.
Don't think so much, she also never told me.
And then the sun sails out of its murky shroud,

which means the moment is over.
Whatever I was given the chance to feel
I should have felt by now.

7

Some ghosts like to smash things,
others are quiet. Some ghosts
are bored, like children on a rainy day,

others get angry. Maybe no one's
reminded them this world is mostly
empty space. Maybe they just want

to be seen once in a while. That's what
I'd want if I were among them—for you
to believe I'm still here, beside you

right now at the window. Of course
this is not yet the poem about love.

*

"Not even close," the man in the road insists.
"Listen," I tell him, "I should go home."
"Are you tired? Would you like to lie down?"

"Yes, I'm tired, and I'd like to lie down."

"I always enjoy a ballad," he says. "Ballads
are underrated these days, repetition as well."

*

A few notes from a piano, and night descends,
as if to say: go ahead, lie down and sleep,

just as anyone unable to finish
the last chapter of a long novel might fold
the corner of a page, and put the book aside,

or leave it open, trusting someone
will lean over and lift it from you.

*

"So I'll leave you now," he says, "or you
leave me, whichever you prefer. They say
Ruskin was a pedophile, but really

he just couldn't get used to a world
that wasn't like a statue, smooth and perfect.

There was something else I wanted to tell you.
Try to remember it later."

*

Cross out the sky with the moon already risen.
Let the trees do what they do at night.
Let the birds sleep safely in their arms.

In the poem entitled "Plant Life" I want
to include the lilac that failed to bloom
this spring, then the extravagant peonies,

the phlox and columbine, and the delicate ferns
in their shifting patterns of shade. Yes,
there's more, and I could ask what else

you'd like me to name, ask you how
I might help with the garden. And still
this would not be the poem about love.

＊

On the radio a choir is singing about flowers
and love. It's spring, they go together.
A soft rain touches the earth when it's needed.

The air is awash with fragrance, and the song
we stop our work to listen to is an old song.
It believes in permanence, and repetition.

No bomb will tear your leg off in this song.
Nor will you lose all your money
and be sent out to beg in the streets. Instead,

many green things will flourish and be praised.
The harvest will be praised, and winter as well,
since this song is designed to accommodate

as much as it can—time to save, time to plan
for what must be saved, all the seasons
arrayed in their appointed order,

which leads us to love, since those who live
in this world, and care for it, care for each other,
and for the ghosts who must be helped to sleep.

Maybe a god watches over it and is pleased,
but the song hasn't mentioned him yet, just the bounty
of the earth, and the men and women who complete it.

Come, sit beside me. Let's listen together until the end.

Acknowledgments

Grateful acknowledgment is made to the following publications in which these poems first appeared.

The Common: "The Major Subjects," "The Mortality of Books," and "Original Sin"

Connotation Press: An Online Artifact: "The Hot Fives and Hot Sevens," "Once, But No Longer," and "Parable of the Windows"

Garbonzo: "The Truth of the Cookie"

Hampden-Sydney Poetry Review: "If I'm Watching You Down in the Garden," "Last Evening," and "The Slamming of a Door Downstairs"

The Idaho Review: "At About This Hour" and "The Weight"

Lake Effect: "I Was Just Wondering"

The Massachusetts Review: "Restoration" and "The Sirens"

Margie: "My Father's Question"

The Missouri Review: "Another Scenario," "If I Knew What He Knew," "The System," and "What I Should Tell You More Often"

The New Ohio Review: "Heroic," "Nothing," and "When Time Slows Down"

Phantom Drift: "Testament"

Plume: "A Couple of Disasters and a Lot of Landscape," "After the Fall of the House of Usher," "Almost, But Never," "A Plain White Envelope" (as "The Summer House"), "It's Not Just Trains," and "So Much More Mournful Than Before"

River Styx: "Last Day on Earth," "Stuff," and "When Mythology Was the Truth"

The Saranac Review: "I Was About To Go To Sleep" and "Ophelia at Home"

Spirituality and Health: "The Beginning of Philosophy"

"Little Bird," in a slightly different version, first appeared in my book *The History of Forgetting* (Penguin, 2009).

"Riddle," in a slightly different version, first appeared in *The Word Exchange: Anglo-Saxon Poems in Translation*, edited by Greg Delanty and Michael Matto (W. W. Norton, 2011).

"A Cup of Water Turns into a Rose" was published as a chapbook by Adastra Press in 2012. Many thanks to Gary Metras.

I would also like to thank Williams College, The MacDowell Colony, and the Corporation of Yaddo for the support and time essential to the making of this collection. Grateful acknowledgment to Yun-Fei Ji for the title, "Mistaking Each Other for Ghosts." Finally, I want to acknowledge my companion and daemon, my bearded collie Molly (1998–2010), who happily stayed with me in my studio when I worked, and eagerly accompanied me on countless walks during which many of these poems were conceived or revised. She should have lived longer. —L. R.

Other books from Tupelo Press

Fasting for Ramadan: Notes from a Spiritual Practice (memoir), Kazim Ali

Pulp Sonnets (poems, with drawings by Amin Mansouri), Tony Barnstone

Another English: Anglophone Poems from Around the World (anthology), edited by Catherine Barnett and Tiphanie Yanique

gentlessness (poems), Dan Beachy-Quick

New Cathay: Contemporary Chinese Poetry (anthology), edited by Ming Di

Calazaza's Delicious Dereliction (poems), Suzanne Dracius, translated by Nancy Naomi Carlson

Gossip and Metaphysics: Russian Modernist Poetry and Prose (anthology), edited by Katie Farris, Ilya Kaminsky, and Valzhyna Mort

The Posthumous Affair (novel), James Friel

Entwined: Three Lyric Sequences (poems), Carol Frost

Poverty Creek Journal (lyric memoir), Thomas Gardner

The Faulkes Chronicle (novel), David Huddle

Darktown Follies (poems), Amaud Jamaul Johnson

Dancing in Odessa (poems), Ilya Kaminsky

A God in the House: Poets Talk About Faith (interviews), edited by Ilya Kaminsky and Katherine Towler

Lucky Fish (poems), Aimee Nezhukumatathil

Ex-Voto (poems), Adélia Prado, translated by Ellen Doré Watson

Intimate: An American Family Photo Album (hybrid memoir), Paisley Rekdal

Thrill-Bent (novel), Jan Richman

The Book of Stones and Angels (poems), Harold Schweizer

Cream of Kohlrabi (stories), Floyd Skloot

The Well Speaks of Its Own Poison (poems), Maggie Smith

The Perfect Life (lyric essays), Peter Stitt

Swallowing the Sea (essays), Lee Upton

Lantern Puzzle (poems), Ye Chun

See our complete list at www.tupelopress.org